Modern Puritan Prayers

40 Attributes of God

Table of Contents

Introduction

I was working at a church-focused tech startup when I first encountered the book The Valley of Vision. A colleague inadvertently introduced me by entering one of its prayers into the system we were building. When I came across it, I loved the reverent tone, focus on God, and scriptural language. Once I learned of its origin, I obtained the book shortly after.

In that season, I enjoyed including those prayers in my morning devotionals. They helped me draw near to the Lord in ways I hadn't for a long time. I would often find a phrase or section to meditate on throughout the day. The truth distilled into those words spoke to my heart.

However, the main problem with historical prayers is that there are, by definition, only so many of them. I began to look for similar collections. I found there were not many in print. Even public domain works were scarce. Coincidentally, this was also around the time that ChatGPT took the world by storm. Out of curiosity, I began to experiment to see if generative AI could be helpful in inspiring more prayers like this.

After much trial and error, I found that large language models can indeed produce the beginnings of prayers in the Puritan style. With polish and editing, they came to life. I began to supplement my own prayer time with these creations, and they inspired and led me toward the Lord in the same manner as those written hundreds of years ago. These are the creations I now share in *Modern Puritan Prayers*.

Any devoted believer will attest that prayer is a matter of the heart. Whether the words are your own, a liturgy, a Psalm, or the writings of another, the goal is to connect with the Father. It's my hope that this collection of prayers will help you do just that.

Ty DeLong

Producer and Editor

The Abundance of God

O Lord of boundless bounty,

Thou who fillest all things with plenteousness,

Thy mercies overflow as rivers in the spring,

Thy gifts are as countless as the stars in the heavens.

In Thy great abundance, thou dost lavish upon us

Riches of grace beyond measure,

Thou dost bestow upon us daily bread,

And thy provision never faileth.

Teach us to see thy hand in every good thing,

To acknowledge thy goodness in all our ways,

May we never cease to praise thee

For the abundance of thy mercy and love.

We long, O Lord, for hearts of gratitude,

That we may offer unto thee the sacrifice of praise,

And with joyful lips declare thy goodness,

For thou art the God of overflowing grace.

Forgive us, O Lord, for our ingratitude,

For our hearts are often unthankful,

We take thy blessings for granted,

And forget the source from whence they come.

Let thy abundance fill us to overflowing,

That we may share thy blessings with others,

And may our lives be a testimony

To the richness of thy love and provision.

O Lord, in thy abundant mercy, hear our prayer,

And grant unto us thy peace,

For in thee alone do we find true satisfaction,

Now and forevermore. Amen.

The Beauty of God

O Sovereign Lord, whose beauty surpasses all,

Thou art the fairest among ten thousand,

The bright and morning star,

Whose glory fills the heavens and the earth.

In thee, O Lord, we behold the splendor of thy majesty,

The beauty of thy holiness,

Thou art clothed in light as with a garment,

And thy radiance shines forth like the noonday sun.

We stand in awe of thy beauty, O Lord,

For thou art the source of all that is lovely and pure,

Thy works declare thy greatness,

And thy creation reflects the beauty of thy handiwork.

Cleanse us, O Lord, for failing to recognize thy beauty,

For our eyes are often blind to thy glory,

Open our eyes, O Lord, to behold thy beauty,

And captivate our hearts with thy loveliness.

We seek, O Lord, hearts of adoration and worship,

That we may glorify thee in all that we do,

And may our lives be a reflection of thy beauty,

For thou art the God of infinite splendor and grace.

Help us to delight in thy beauty, O Lord,

And may we never cease to praise thee,

For thou art the fairest among ten thousand,

And thy beauty endures forever.

O Lord, in thy boundless beauty, hear our prayer,

And let thy glory fill the earth,

For thou art the God of all beauty,

Whose radiance shines over all, now and forevermore. Amen.

The Compassion of God

O Sovereign Lord, whose compassions fail not,

Thou art a God of tender mercy,

Whose heart overflows with love towards thy children.

Thou dost look upon us with eyes of compassion,

And thy heart is moved with pity for our frailty.

In our distress, thou art our refuge,

In our sorrow, thou art our comforter,

Thou dost draw near to the broken-hearted,

And dost bind up their wounds with thy gentle touch.

In thy mercy, O Lord, grant us hearts of compassion,

That we may bear one another's burdens,

And be ministers of thy grace to those in need,

As thou hast commanded us.

Let thy compassion be our guide,

Leading us in paths of righteousness,

And may we never forget the depth of thy love,

Which surpasses all understanding.

Absolve us, O Lord, from our hardness of heart,

From our lack of compassion towards others,

Teach us to love as thou hast loved us,

And to show mercy as thou hast shown mercy unto us.

O Lord, in thy boundless compassion, hear our prayer,

And let thy mercy shine upon us,

For thou art the God of unfailing compassion,

Now and forevermore. Amen.

The Creativity of God

O Sovereign Creator, whose handiwork declares thy glory,
Thou art the source of all wonder,
In thy wisdom, thou hast fashioned the heavens and the earth,
And thy creativity knows no bounds.

Thou art the master artist, painting the hues of dawn,
Sculpting the mountains with thy mighty hands,
And crafting every creature with precision and care.

We marvel at the wonders of thy creation,
And stand in awe of thy infinite mind,
For thou dost reveal thyself in every flower that blooms,
And every bird that sings praises to thy name.

We desire, O Lord, hearts of wonder and gratitude,
That we may rejoice in thy creativity,
And give thanks for the richness of thy creation,
Which reflects the glory of thy presence.

Have mercy, O Lord, when we fail to recognize thy handiwork,

For taking thy creation for granted,

Teach us to see thee in all things,

And to appreciate the beauty of thy design.

Help us be inspired by thy creativity,

And use our gifts and talents to glorify thee,

For thou art the God of all creativity,

And to thee be all honor and praise forevermore.

O Lord, in thy boundless creativity, hear our prayer,

And let thy Spirit inspire us to new heights,

For thou art the source of all inspiration,

Now and forevermore. Amen.

The Eternality of God

O Eternal and timeless God,

Thou art the Alpha and the Omega,

The beginning and the end,

Thy years have no end, and thy throne is forever established.

Before the foundation of the world, thou wast,

And after all things pass away, thou shalt remain,

Thy existence knows no bounds,

And thy glory fills all eternity.

Pardon us, O Lord, for our finite understanding,

For trying to comprehend thee with mortal minds,

Teach us to stand in awe of thy majesty,

And to trust in thy eternal purposes.

In thee, O Lord, we find our refuge,

For thou art our rock and our fortress,

In thee, there is no shadow of turning,

And thy presence endures from generation to generation.

We shall find our rest in thee, O Eternal God,

And we shall dwell in the shadow of thy wings forever,

For thou art the unchanging One,

Who reigns over all, now and for all eternity.

Instill into us, O Lord, hearts of wisdom and humility,

That we may acknowledge thee as the Ancient of Days,

And bow before thee in reverence and awe,

For thou art the God who was, and is, and is to come.

O Lord, in thy eternal love, hear our prayer,

And let thy name be praised throughout all ages,

For thou art the Alpha and the Omega,

The beginning and the end, forevermore. Amen.

The Faithfulness of God

O Faithful and True God,

Thou art the steadfast anchor of our souls,

Whose promises never fail,

And whose faithfulness endures forever.

Thou hast been faithful to thy people throughout the ages,

In times of trial and tribulation,

Thou hast upheld us with thy mighty hand,

And never once hast thou forsaken us.

In thee, O Lord, we find our security,

For thou art the rock of our salvation,

Thy faithfulness is a shield and a buckler,

And under thy wings, we find refuge.

Have compassion, O Lord, for our wavering faith,

For doubting thy promises and thy providence,

Teach us to trust in thee with all our hearts,

And to lean not on our own understanding.

Bless us, O Lord, with hearts of steadfastness,

That we may hold fast to thy word,

And walk in obedience to thy commands,

For thou art the God who is ever faithful.

May we never forget thy faithfulness, O Lord,

And may we proclaim thy faithfulness to all generations,

For thy promises are ever true,

And thy faithfulness endures to all eternity.

O Lord, in thy faithfulness, hear our prayer,

And let thy name be praised throughout all the earth,

For thou art the faithful and true God,

Who reigns over all, now and forevermore. Amen.

The Forgiveness of God

O Merciful Father, whose compassions fail not,

Thou art the fountain of forgiveness,

Whose grace flows freely to the repentant soul,

And whose mercy knows no bounds.

We come before thee, O Lord, with contrite hearts,

Confessing our sins and transgressions,

For we have fallen short of thy glory,

And have wandered far from thy righteous path.

But thou, O Lord, art rich in mercy,

And abounding in steadfast love,

Thou dost not deal with us according to our sins,

Nor repay us according to our iniquities.

We long, O Lord, for hearts of repentance and humility,

That we may turn from our wicked ways,

And seek thy face with sincerity and earnestness,

For thou art the God who forgives all our sins.

Cleanse us, O Lord, of our rebellion and stubbornness,

For our hearts are prone to wander,

Lead us back to thy loving embrace,

And restore unto us the joy of thy salvation.

Let us never take for granted the depth of thy forgiveness,

But may we rejoice in the mercy and grace thou hast shown us,

For thou art the God who pardons our iniquities,

And casts our sins into the depths of the sea.

O Lord, in thy abundant mercy, hear our prayer,

And let thy forgiveness flow like a river,

For thou art the God of unfailing grace,

Who forgives the penitent, now and forevermore. Amen.

The Generosity of God

O Gracious and Bountiful God,

Thou art the giver of every good and perfect gift,

Whose generosity knows no bounds,

And whose blessings are poured out upon us overflowing.

Thou dost provide for our every need,

And thou dost lavish upon us thy grace and mercy,

Thy hand is open wide to satisfy the desires of our hearts,

And thou dost bless us beyond measure.

Purify us, O Lord, from our ingratitude,

For our hearts are often unthankful,

We take thy blessings for granted,

And fail to recognize the source from which they come

In thy great generosity, thou hast given us life and breath,

And all things necessary for our sustenance,

Thou dost shower us with blessings from heaven above,

And thy provision never ceases.

We desire, O Lord, hearts of gratitude and generosity,

That we may share thy blessings with others,

And be instruments of thy love and mercy in the world,

For thou art the God of overflowing grace.

Teach us to be mindful of thy generosity, O Lord,

And to give thanks for thy goodness each day,

May we never cease to praise thee

For the abundance of thy provision and grace.

May our lives be a testimony to thy generosity,

And may we never forget the riches of thy kindness,

For thou art the generous giver of every good gift,

Now and forevermore. Amen.

The Glory of God

O Sovereign Lord, whose glory fills the heavens,

Thou art clothed in majesty and splendor,

Thy greatness is beyond all comprehension,

And thy power is without measure.

We bow in awe of thy glory, O Lord,

For thou art the King of kings and Lord of lords,

Thy throne is established in righteousness,

And thy kingdom shall endure forever.

In thy presence, O Lord, we behold thy glory,

And we are humbled before thee,

For thou art the Creator of all things,

And in thee, all things hold together.

Grant us, O Lord, hearts of reverence and adoration,

That we may worship thee in spirit and in truth,

And give unto thee the glory due thy name,

For thou art the God of all glory.

Forgive us, O Lord, for our pride and arrogance,

For we have exalted ourselves above thee,

Teach us to bow before thy majesty,

And to acknowledge thee as the glorious ruler of the universe.

Let our lives be a reflection of thy glory,

And may we proclaim thy greatness to all the earth,

For thou art the Alpha and the Omega,

The beginning and the end, the first and the last.

O Lord, in thy glorious majesty, hear our prayer,

And let thy name be exalted above all others,

For thou art the King of glory,

Who reigns over all, now and forevermore. Amen.

The Goodness of God

O Most Perfect and Good God,

Thou art the essence of goodness,

Whose righteousness is flawless,

And through whom we know what is good.

In thee, O Lord, we find our every need fulfilled,

For thou art the giver of every good and perfect gift,

Thy goodness surrounds us like a shield,

And thy mercy endures forever.

Absolve, O Lord, from our lack of goodness,

For our hearts are by nature evil,

Help us to laud thy goodness in all things,

And to give thanks for the enlightenment of thy word.

We marvel at the purity of thy perfection,

For thou showest us all that is praiseworthy,

Thou dost satisfy all the hungers of our souls,

And quench the thirst of our spirits with thy living waters.

We seek, O Lord, hearts aligned with thy goodness,
That we may declare thy truth to all generations,
And testify to thy righteousness and love,
For thou art the only good God.

May we never cease to marvel at thy light, O Lord,
And may we find our joy in thee alone,
For thou art the source of all good,
And to thee is all honor and glory due.

O Lord, in thy boundless goodness, hear our prayer,
And let thy goodness shine upon us,
For thou art the God of unfailing love,
Now and forevermore. Amen.

The Grace of God

O Sovereign Lord, whose grace is boundless,

Thou art patient beyond measure,

Whose mercy reaches to the heavens,

And whose love endures forever.

In thy grace, O Lord, we find our salvation,

For thou hast poured out thy favor upon us,

And redeemed us from the power of sin and death,

Through the precious blood of thy Son, Jesus Christ.

Thy grace is our strength in times of weakness,

And our comfort in times of sorrow,

For thou art the God who gives grace abundantly,

To all who call upon thy name.

Help us, O Lord, to know true gratitude,

That we may humbly receive thy grace,

And share it with others who are in need,

For thou art the God of all grace.

Have mercy on us, O Lord, for our indifference,

For taking thy grace for granted,

Teach us to treasure the gift of salvation,

And to live lives worthy of the calling we have received.

We marvel at the richness of thy grace, O Lord,

For thou hast lavished upon us blessings untold,

And bestowed upon us the gift of eternal life,

Through faith in thy beloved Son.

O Lord, in thy boundless grace, hear our prayer,

And let thy grace fill our hearts,

For thou art the God of all grace,

Now and forevermore. Amen.

The Guidance of God

O Sovereign Lord, whose wisdom is unsearchable,
Thou art the guide of our steps,
Whose hand leads us in paths of righteousness,
And whose light shines upon our way.

In thee, O Lord, we find our direction,
For thou art the compass of our souls,
Thy word is a lamp unto our feet,
And a light unto our path.

Forgive us, O Lord, for our folly and pride,
For our hearts are prone to wander,
Teach us to submit to thy will,
And to follow thy leading with humble obedience.

Guide us, O Lord, in thy truth and righteousness,
Lead us by thy Spirit into all truth,
And keep us from the snares of the evil one,
Who seeks to lead us astray.

Instill in us, O Lord, hearts of prudence and wisdom,

That we may discern thy will in all things,

And walk in the way that leads to life,

For thou art the God who guides us with thy counsel.

Let us never stray from thy paths, O Lord,

But follow thee faithfully all the days of our lives,

For thou art the Shepherd of our souls,

And in thy direction, we find rest and peace.

O Wonderful Counselor, hear our prayer,

And guide us safely through the tribulations of this world,

For thou art the God who leads us in paths of righteousness,

Now and forevermore. Amen.

The Healing of God

O Glorious Physician of our souls,

Thou art the great Healer of our infirmities,

Whose touch brings restoration and wholeness,

And whose grace heals the broken-hearted.

We come before thee, O Lord, with our wounds and ailments,

Seeking thy healing touch and tender care,

For we are weary and burdened,

And in need of thy divine intervention.

Thou, O Lord, art the balm of Gilead,

Whose healing power knows no bounds,

Thou dost bring comfort to the afflicted,

And bind up the wounds of the broken.

Strengthen us, O Lord, in our lack of faith,

When doubting thy power to heal and restore,

Teach us to trust in thy sovereign will,

And to surrender our lives into thy loving hands.

We desire, O Lord, hearts of faith and patience,

That we may wait upon thee in expectation,

And receive thy healing touch in thy time,

For thou art the God who heals all our diseases.

We praise thee for thy healing grace,

And we testify to thy goodness and mercy,

For thou art the God who brings healing to the nations,

And whose compassion knows no end.

O Lord of boundless restoration, hear our prayer,

And let thy healing power be made manifest in our lives,

For thou art the great Physician,

Who renews all, now and forevermore. Amen.

The Holiness of God

O Holy and Righteous God,

Thou art clothed in unapproachable light,

Thy holiness is beyond measure,

And thy purity shines forth like the noonday sun.

Thou art the thrice-holy One,

Before whom angels veil their faces,

And the heavens declare thy glory,

For thou art the King of kings and Lord of lords.

In thy presence, O Lord, we tremble,

For thou art a consuming fire,

And none can stand before thee in their own righteousness,

For all have sinned and fallen short of thy glory.

Grant unto us, O Lord, hearts of purity and holiness,

That we may walk blamelessly before thee,

And reflect thy holiness in all we do,

For thou art the God who calls us to be holy as thou art holy.

May we tremble at thy word, O Holy God,

And may we revere thee in all our ways,

For thou art the Holy One of Israel,

And thy name is to be feared above all names.

Purify us, O Lord, from unholy actions and thoughts,

For our hearts are deceitful above all things,

Cleanse us from all unrighteousness,

And create in us a clean heart, O God.

O Lord, in thy holiness, hear our prayer,

And may all creation bow before thee,

For thou art the Holy and Mighty One,

Who reigns over all, now and forevermore. Amen.

The Immanence of God

O Eternal and Immanent God,

Thou art the ever-present One,

Whose Spirit fills the heavens and the earth,

And whose presence permeates all things.

Thou art not far from us, O Lord,

For in thee we live, and move, and have our being,

Thy hand sustains us from moment to moment,

And thy spirit dwells within our hearts.

In thee, O Lord, we find our refuge,

For thou art our hiding place and our shield,

Thy presence surrounds us like a mighty fortress,

And in thy shadow, we find rest and peace.

Cleanse us, O Lord, of our blindness and ignorance,

Of failing to recognize thy presence in our midst,

Open our eyes to behold thee,

And awaken our hearts to feel thy nearness.

Let us never forget thy immanence, O Lord,

But may we be ever mindful of thy presence with us,

For thou art the God who walks beside us,

And in thee, we find our strength and our joy.

We long, O Lord, for hearts of sensitivity and awareness,

That we may discern thy hand in all things,

And walk in communion with thee day by day,

For thou art the God who permeates all.

O Lord, in thy abiding presence, hear our prayer,

And let thy spirit fill us with thy peace,

For thou art the God who is always near,

Now and forevermore. Amen.

The Immutability of God

O Immutable God, unchanging and eternal,

Thou art the Rock of Ages,

Whose steadfastness knows no alteration,

And whose word endures from everlasting to everlasting.

In thee, O Lord, we find our security,

For thou art the same yesterday, today, and forever,

Thy purposes stand firm throughout all generations,

And thy word remains true for all eternity.

Have mercy on us, O Lord, for our inconstancy,

For doubting thy steadfastness and thy sovereignty,

Teach us to trust in thee with all our hearts,

And to rest in the assurance of thy unchanging nature.

Thou hast been our refuge and our strength,

In times of trouble and uncertainty,

Thou hast upheld us with thy mighty hand,

And never once hast thou wavered in thy love for us.

We beseech thee, O Lord, for hearts of constancy,

That we may cling to thy promises with unwavering faith,

And walk in obedience to thy will,

For thou art the God who never changes.

May we find our peace in thee, O Immutable God,

And may we rejoice in the unchanging nature of thy character,

For thou art the Rock upon which we build our lives,

And in thee, we find our strength and our salvation.

O Lord, in thy unchanging perfection, hear our prayer,

And let thy name be praised throughout all generations,

For thou art the same yesterday, today, and forever,

The eternal and consistent God. Amen.

The Jealousy of God

O Mighty and Jealous God,

Thou art a consuming fire,

Whose desire for your people burns with holy zeal,

And whose passion for righteousness knows no bounds.

Thou art the jealous guardian of thy glory,

And thou wilt not share thy worship with any other,

For thou alone art worthy of all praise,

And thou alone art deserving of our devotion.

Absolve us, O Lord, from our idolatry,

From seeking after other gods and pursuing earthly pleasures,

Teach us to love thee with all our heart, soul, and strength,

And to worship thee in spirit and in truth.

Let us never provoke thy jealousy, O Lord,

But let us honor thee as the one true God,

And give thee the worship and adoration that is due thy name,

For thou art the jealous God who will not share his glory.

We need, O Lord, hearts of purity and devotion,

That we may serve thee with singleness of heart,

And be zealous for thy honor and glory,

For thou art the God who is protective of his people.

O Lord, in thy righteous love, hear our prayer,

And let thy jealousy be a consuming fire within us,

That burns away all that is not pleasing in thy sight,

And purifies us to be vessels of honor for thy use. Amen.

The Justice of God

O Righteous Judge of all the earth,
Thou art the embodiment of perfect justice,
Whose judgments are true and righteous altogether,
And whose ways are beyond reproach.

We bow before thee, O Lord, with reverence and awe,
Acknowledging thy just rule over all creation,
And thy authority to execute perfect judgment.

Thou hast set forth thy law as a standard of holiness,
And thou dost require obedience from thy people,
Yet we confess, O Lord, that we have fallen short,
And have transgressed thy holy commandments.

But thou, O God, art not swayed by partiality or bribery,
Thou dost judge with equity and impartiality,
And thou wilt render to every man according to his deeds.

Pardon us, O Lord, for our sins and transgressions,

For the ways in which we have rebelled against thy perfect law,

Fill us, O Lord, with hearts of repentance and contrition,

That we may turn from our wicked ways and seek thy mercy.

May thy justice be tempered with mercy, O Lord,

And may thy grace abound toward those who humbly repent,

But let thy justice be swift and sure against the unrepentant,

For thou art the God who will by no means clear the guilty.

O Lord, in thy righteous judgment, hear our prayer,

And let thy justice reign throughout all the earth,

For thou art the true and only Judge of all,

Who rules now and forevermore. Amen.

The Kindness of God

O Gracious and Kind God,

Thou art the epitome of kindness and compassion,

Whose tender mercies are new every morning,

And whose love knows no end.

Thou dost lavish thy kindness upon us,

Pouring out blessings like rain from heaven,

And providing for our every need with abundant generosity.

In thee, O Lord, we find refuge and solace,

For thou art the gentle Shepherd who leads us,

And the caring Father who watches over his children.

Have mercy, O Lord, for our indifference and selfishness,

For we often fail to recognize thy goodwill towards us,

We set our minds on things below,

And shun thy merciful entreaties.

May we never cease to marvel at thy lovingkindness,

And may we proclaim thy benevolence to all who will hear,

For thou hast entered our lowly state in thy Son,

To redeem us from the pit of our destruction.

O Lord, in thy wonderful kindness, hear our prayer,

And let thy goodness shine forth in our lives,

For thou art the God who loveth us first,

Now and forevermore. Amen.

The Kingship of God

O Sovereign King, whose dominion is everlasting,

Thou art the ruler of heaven and earth,

Whose throne is established in righteousness,

And whose scepter is one of justice and mercy.

Thou art the King of kings and Lord of lords,

Before thee, every knee shall bow,

And every tongue shall confess thy majesty,

For thou art the supreme ruler over all creation.

In thy sovereignty, O Lord, we find our security,

For thou art the Almighty who reigns on high,

Thy kingdom is an everlasting kingdom,

And thy dominion knows no end.

Fill us, O Lord, with hearts of obedience and humility,

That we may serve our holy King with reverence and awe,

And seek thy kingdom above all else,

For thou art the King who brings peace and righteousness.

We beg forgiveness, O Lord, for our rebellion and pride,

For we often pursue our own kingdoms,

Teach us to submit to thy rule and authority,

And to acknowledge thee as the rightful King of our lives.

May thy kingdom come, O Lord,

And thy will be done on earth as it is in heaven,

And may we, thy subjects, proclaim thy rule

With hearts full of praise and adoration.

O Lord, in thy kingly majesty, hear our prayer,

And let thy kingdom be established,

For thou art the true King,

Who reigns over all, now and forevermore. Amen.

The Love of God

O Loving Father,

Thou art the embodiment of love itself,

Whose affection for thy children knows no bounds,

And whose compassion endures for all eternity.

Thou hast loved us with an everlasting love,

Even before the foundations of the world were laid,

Thou didst set thy affection upon us,

And dost draw us unto thyself with cords of love.

In thy great love, thou didst send thy Son,

To redeem us from sin and death,

He bore our sins upon the cross,

And shed his precious blood for our salvation.

Let thy love be the guiding force in our lives,

Leading us in paths of righteousness and peace,

And may we always marvel at the riches of thy love,

Which surpasses all understanding.

Forgive us, O Lord, for our failure to return thy love,

For our hearts are often cold and indifferent,

Open our eyes to behold the depth of thy love for us,

And melt our hearts with thy tender affection.

We beseech thee, O Lord, for hearts of devotion,

That we may love thee with all our heart, soul, and mind,

And love our neighbors as ourselves,

For he who does not love does not know thee.

O Lord, in thy boundless love, hear our prayer,

And let us know the warmth of thy embrace,

For thou art the God of unfailing love,

Who reigns over all, now and forevermore. Amen.

The Majesty of God

O Mighty and Majestic God,
Thou art clothed in splendor and adorned with glory,
Thy throne is established in the heavens,
And the earth trembles at thy presence.

Thou art the Everlasting King,
Before whom every knee shall bow,
And every tongue shall confess thy name,
For thou art exalted above all.

In thee, O Lord, we behold thy majesty,
In the wonders of creation and the beauty of thy handiwork,
Thou dost reveal thy glory to all who have eyes to see,
And hearts to perceive thy greatness.

Grant unto us, O Lord, a comprehension of thy glory,
That we may bow before thee in worship and adoration,
And declare thy greatness to all the earth,
For thou art the God of unmatched majesty.

Even thy majestic name fills us with wonder and awe,

And we shall never cease to praise thee,

For all thou art,

And all thou hast done.

Have compassion, O Lord, for our small thoughts of thee,

For our failure to understand the magnitude of thy majesty,

Teach us to approach thee with reverence and awe,

And to worship thee in spirit and in truth.

O Lord, in thy majestic splendor, hear our prayer,

And let thy glory fill the earth,

For thou art the Infinite God,

Whose splendor is forever and ever. Amen.

The Mercy of God

O Merciful Lord, whose love endures forever,

Thou art the God of compassion and grace,

Whose tender mercies are new every morning,

And whose lovingkindness knows no end.

In thee, O Lord, we find our reassurance,

For thou art the fountain of all mercy,

Thy compassion is boundless,

And thy grace abounds to the greatest of sinners.

We come before thee, O Lord, with humble hearts,

Acknowledging our unworthiness and our sinfulness,

But trusting in thy abundant mercy and forgiveness,

Which thou dost freely offer to all who call upon thy name.

Have mercy on us, O Lord, for our transgressions,

For we have sinned against thee in thought, word, and deed,

Yet thou, O Lord, art quick to forgive,

And thy mercy triumphs over judgment.

We desire, O Lord, hearts of mercy,

That we may act justly and love mercy,

And proclaim thy kindness to all generations,

For the merciful shall receive mercy.

Let us never lose sight of thy mercy, O Lord,

But may it be ever before us as a beacon of hope,

Leading us to repentance and renewal,

And guiding us in the paths of righteousness.

O Lord, in thy boundless mercy, hear our prayer,

And let thy compassion rest upon us,

For thou art the God of all grace,

Who longs to show mercy to all, now and forevermore. Amen.

The Omnipotence of God

O All-Powerful God,

Thou art the omnipotent Ruler of the universe,

Whose power knows no limits,

And whose strength is beyond comprehension.

Thou didst speak, and the heavens were formed,

Thou didst command, and the earth came into being,

All things were created by thy mighty word,

And nothing is too difficult for thee.

In thee, O Lord, we find our strength and our refuge,

For thou art the Almighty,

Thy arm is not shortened, nor thy power diminished,

And thou art able to do exceedingly above all that we imagine.

We desire, O Lord, hearts of confidence and courage,

That we may face every trial and temptation with boldness,

Knowing that nothing can stand against thee,

For we serve the God whose power is over all.

May we never forget the greatness of thy strength,

But may we stand in awe of thy majesty and might,

And may we proclaim thy omnipotence to all,

For thou art the supreme and all-powerful God.

Strengthen us, O Lord, in our feeble faith,

For we doubt thy ability to accomplish thy purposes,

Teach us to trust in thy perfect will,

And to rest in the assurance of thy sovereignty.

O Lord, in thy omnipotence, hear our prayer,

And let thy great name be exalted among the nations,

For thou art the only Almighty God,

Who reigns over all, now and forevermore. Amen.

The Omnipresence of God

O Sovereign Lord, whose presence permeates thy creation,

Thou art the God who is ever near,

Whose eyes behold all the works of men,

And whose Spirit encompasses the heavens and the earth.

Thou art not confined to temples made with hands,

Nor limited by time or space,

But thou dost dwell in the hearts of thy people,

And thy glory fills the highest heavens.

Nothing escapes your gaze, O Lord,

For thou art always with us,

Thy presence goes before us like a pillar of fire,

And thy Spirit guides us in the paths of righteousness.

Cleanse us, O Lord, from our forgetfulness of thy presence,

For we often go about our days as though thou wert far off,

Teach us to be mindful of thy nearness,

And to walk in the light of thy presence.

Let us never seek to stray from thy presence, O Lord,

But may we abide in thee as branches in the vine,

For thou art the source of all life and strength,

And apart from thee, we can do nothing.

We seek, O Lord, a spirit of awareness and reverence,

That we may live our lives as in thy sight,

And seek thy face in all that we do,

For thou art the God who is ever present.

O Lord, we know thou art all around,

Let thy Spirit dwell richly within us as we pray,

For thou art the God who is always near,

Now and forevermore. Amen.

The Omniscience of God

O Omniscient and Infinite God,

Thou who art the Knower of all things,

Whose wisdom surpasses all understanding,

And whose knowledge is without limit.

Thou hast searched us and known us,

Thou art acquainted with all our ways,

There is not a thought in our hearts

That is hidden from thee.

In thy omniscience, O Lord,

Thou dost see the end from the beginning,

Thou knowest the secrets of the universe,

And the mysteries of our souls are laid bare before thee.

We desire, O Lord, hearts of wisdom and humility,

That we may acknowledge our shortsightedness,

And trust in thy omniscient care,

Knowing that thou art the God who sees and knows all.

We take comfort in thy omniscience, O Lord,

And find peace in the knowledge

That nothing escapes thy notice,

And that thou art always with us, directing our steps.

Pardon us, O Lord, for our presumption,

For thinking that we can hide from thy sight,

Teach us to walk in the fear of the Lord,

And to acknowledge thee in all our ways.

O Lord, in thy infinite sight, hear our prayer,

And let thy omniscience be our confidence,

For thou art the God who knoweth all,

Now and forevermore. Amen.

The Patience of God

O Longsuffering and Patient God,
Thou art the epitome of endurance and forbearance,
Whose patience extends throughout all generations,
And whose longsuffering endures forever.

Thou dost wait patiently for the wayward sinner to return,
And dost bear with our shortcomings and failings,
Thou dost not hastily condemn us to destruction,
But dost extend thy hand of mercy to lead us to repentance.

In thee, O Lord, we find our perfect example,
For thou dost patiently work in our lives,
Molding us into vessels of honor fit for thy service,
And patiently bear with our weaknesses.

Forgive us, O Lord, for our impatience and lack of trust,
For we often grow weary in waiting for thy timing,
Teach us to wait upon thee with forbearance,
And to trust in thy perfect plan for our lives.

We long, O Lord, for hearts of patience and humility,

That we may learn to bear with one another,

And to surrender our will to thy sovereign hand,

For thou worketh all things according to thy purposes.

May we never take for granted thy patience toward us,

But may we marvel at thy longsuffering and grace,

For thou doth wait patiently for us to come to repentance,

And who rejoices over the return of the prodigal.

O Lord, in thy infinite patience, hear our prayer,

And let thy patience be our example and inspiration,

For thou art slow to anger and abounding in mercy,

And patient in all, now and forevermore. Amen.

The Peace of God

O Sovereign Lord, whose peace surpasses all understanding,

Thou art the Prince of Peace,

Whose presence brings tranquility to troubled hearts,

And whose word calms the raging storms.

In thee, O Lord, we find our rest,

For thou art the source of true peace,

Thy peace is not of this world,

But a peace that flows from the depths of thy being.

We repent, O Lord, for seeking peace in the things of the world,

For our hearts are restless until they find their rest in thee,

Teach us to abide in thy peace,

And to trust in thy unfailing love.

Instill in us, O Lord, hearts of serenity and trust,

That we may cast all our cares upon thee,

And find refuge in the shadow of thy wings,

For thou art the God who gives peace to the weary soul.

Let thy peace reign in our hearts,

And may it overflow to those around us,

That they may see the peace that surpasses all understanding,

And be drawn to thee, the giver of peace.

O Lord, in thy boundless serenity, hear our prayer,

And let thy peace rule in our hearts,

For thou art the God of peace,

Who reigns over all, now and forevermore. Amen.

The Perfection of God

O Most Holy and Perfect God,

Thou art the embodiment of purity and righteousness,

In thee, there is no shadow of turning,

And thy perfection shines forth in all thy ways.

Thou art the unblemished Lamb,

Spotless and without fault,

Thy ways are perfect, and thy judgments are just,

And in thy presence, there is no room for sin or imperfection.

We bow before thee, O Lord,

In awe of thy holiness and majesty,

For our blemishes are manifold,

And thy perfection knows no bounds.

Purify us, O Lord, for we are wholly corrupt,

Our hearts are deceitful above all things,

And we often fall short of thy glory,

But thou, O God, art faithful and just to forgive us our sins.

Help us strive for perfection, O Lord,

Not in our own strength, but in the power of thy Spirit,

And may we be conformed to the image of thy Son,

Who is the perfect representation of thy glory.

We long, O Lord, for hearts of purity and righteousness,

That we may stand blamelessly before thee,

And reflect thy perfection in all that we do,

For thou art the God who calls us to be holy as thou art holy.

O Lord, in thy perfect holiness, hear our prayer,

And let thy purity radiate in all creation,

For thou art the Holy One of Israel,

Who reigns over all, now and forevermore. Amen.

The Providence of God

O Sovereign Lord, whose providence governs all things,

Thou art the Almighty Ruler of the universe,

Whose hand guides the course of history,

And whose wisdom orders all events according to thy will.

In thy providence, O Lord, we find our peace,

For thou art the Shepherd who leads us beside still waters,

And the Protector who watches over us day and night,

Thy providential care sustains us in every trial.

We acknowledge, O Lord, our finite understanding,

And humbly submit to thy sovereign rule,

For thou alone art wise and just in all thy ways,

And thy purposes cannot be thwarted by the schemes of men.

Grant unto us, O Lord, hearts of faith and submission,

That we may rest in the assurance of thy sovereign control,

And rejoice in knowing that all things work together for good,

To those who love thee and are called according to thy purpose.

Have mercy on us, O Lord, for our lack of trust,

For our hearts are often filled with fear and anxiety,

Teach us to lean not on our own understanding,

But to trust in thy providence with all our hearts.

We shall never lose sight of thy providential care, O Lord,

But continually acknowledge thy hand at work in our lives,

For thou art the God who orders our steps,

And meets our every need.

O Lord, in thy providence, hear our prayer,

And let us see thy hand at work,

For thou art the author and perfecter of our faith,

Who provides for all, now and forevermore. Amen.

The Redemption of God

O Sovereign Redeemer,
Lamb of God who taketh away the sins of the world,
Thou hast redeemed us from the bondage of sin,
And purchased our freedom with thy precious blood.

Thou hast called us out of darkness into thy marvelous light,
And set our feet upon the rock of salvation,
Thou hast clothed us with garments of righteousness,
And made us heirs of thy kingdom forevermore.

We marvel at the wonders of thy redemption,
For thou hast saved us from the power of death,
And given us the gift of eternal life,
Thou hast triumphed over sin and grave,
And seated at the right hand of the Father.

May thy redemption be our song of praise,
And may we never cease to give thanks for thy great love,
For thou art the Redeemer of our souls,
Who has pulled us from the depths.

We seek, O Lord, hearts of humility and gratitude,

That we may never boast except in the cross of Christ,

And may we proclaim thy redemption to all who are lost,

For thou art the God who saves to the uttermost.

Absolve us, O Lord, from our forgetfulness and indifference,

From failing to remember the price of our redemption,

Teach us to treasure the gift of salvation,

And to live each day in grateful obedience to thy will.

O Lord, in thy boundless redemption, hear our prayer,

And let thy name be praised throughout all eternity,

For thou art the only Redeemer,

The restorer of all, now and forevermore. Amen.

The Righteousness of God

O Righteous and Holy God,

Thou art the essence of purity and perfection,

All of thy ways are right,

And thy goodness shines forth like the noonday sun.

Thou art clothed in splendor and majesty,

And thy throne is established in rectitude and justice,

Thou art the righteous judge of all the earth,

And thy word is perfect and true.

We come before thee, O Lord, with hearts bowed in reverence,

Acknowledging our own sinfulness and unworthiness,

For we have fallen short of thy glorious standard,

And have transgressed thy holy law.

But thou, O Lord, art the source of all righteousness,

And in thy mercy, thou dost offer forgiveness and redemption,

Through the sacrifice of thy Son, Jesus Christ,

Who bore our sins upon the cross.

We desire, O Lord, hearts of obedience and holiness,

That we may reflect thy righteousness in all that we do,

And be a testimony to thy grace and mercy,

For thou art the God who has revealed what is right.

Purify us, O Lord, from our disobedience and rebellion,

And cleanse us from all iniquity,

May we be clothed in the righteousness of Christ,

And walk blamelessly before thee all the days of our lives.

Let thy righteousness be our guide and our delight,

And may we seek to honor thee in all things,

For thou art the upright ruler,

Who cannot and will not err.

O Lord, in thy righteousness, hear our prayer,

And let thy greatness be exalted in all the earth,

For thou art the God of holiness and truth,

Who reigns over all, now and forevermore. Amen.

The Salvation of God

O Sovereign Lord, whose salvation is our only hope,

Thou art the author and finisher of our faith,

Whose love compelled thee to send thy Son

To redeem us from the bondage of sin and death.

In thee alone do we find our rescue,

For thou art the Rock of our salvation,

Thy grace is our shield and our strength,

And thy mercy endures forever.

Forgive us, O Lord, for our sins and transgressions,

For we daily need thy salvation from this body of death,

But thou, O God, art rich in mercy,

And dost offer cleansing to all who call upon thy name.

We approach thee, O Lord, with humble hearts,

Acknowledging our need for thy saving power,

For we are lost and without hope apart from thee,

But in thy mercy, thou dost freely offer us the gift of salvation.

Create in us, O Lord, renewed hearts,

That we may turn from our wicked ways

And trust in thy Son, Jesus Christ, as our Savior and Lord,

For in him alone is salvation found.

We shall always marvel at the wonder of thy grace,

And proclaim the gospel of salvation to all nations,

For thou art the God who saves,

And to thee belong all honor and praise.

O Lord, in thy saving power, hear our prayer,

And let thy salvation be known to all the earth,

For thou art the God who delivers us,

Now and forevermore. Amen.

The Sovereignty of God

O Almighty and Sovereign God,

Thou art the ruler over the universe,

Whose throne is established in forever,

And whose dominion knows no end.

Thou dost reign over all things,

From the highest heavens to the deepest depths,

And nothing can thwart thy sovereign will,

For thou art the God who holds all things in thy hands.

In thy sovereignty, O Lord, we find our peace,

For thou art the master of every circumstance,

And thy purposes are sure and unchanging,

Even in the midst of turmoil and chaos.

May we never doubt thy all-encompassing rule, O Lord,

But may we rest in the knowledge that thou art in control,

And that nothing can separate us from thy love,

For thou dost work all things according to thy will.

Remove from us, O Lord, our pride and arrogance,

For thinking that we can control our own destiny,

Teach us to submit to thy sovereign rule,

And to trust in thy wisdom and providence.

Place in us, O Lord, hearts of humility and surrender,

That we may bow before thee in awe and reverence,

And acknowledge thee as wholly sovereign,

For thou art the God who reigns over all.

O Lord, in thy sovereignty, hear our prayer,

And let thy will be done on earth as it is in heaven,

For thy purposes shall always be fulfilled,

Both now and forevermore. Amen.

The Sufficiency of God

O Sovereign Lord, whose sufficiency knows no bounds,

Thou art the inexhaustible source of all good things,

In thee, there is no lack or deficiency,

For thou art the God who provides abundantly for thy people.

Thou art our portion and our strength,

Our rock and our fortress in times of trouble,

In thee, we find all that we need,

And in thee, we are complete.

We repent, O Lord, for seeking joy in earthly treasures,

For chasing after the fleeting pleasures of this world,

Teach us to find our satisfaction in thee alone,

And to trust in thy sufficiency for all our needs.

We long, O Lord, for hearts of contentment and gratitude,

That we may be satisfied with thy provision,

And may we always give thanks for thy abundant blessings,

Which far surpass our deserts.

Let us rest in the assurance of thy sufficiency,

Knowing that in thee, we lack nothing,

And may we live our lives in obedience to thy will,

Trusting that thy provision is always enough.

O Lord, in thy boundless sufficiency, hear our prayer,

And let thy hand sustain us through all the trials of life,

For thou art the God who satisfies the hungry soul,

And fills the longing heart with good things.

Now and forevermore. Amen.

The Sustenance of God

O Gracious Provider, whose hand sustains all creation,

Thou holdest all things together,

Thy bounty never ceases,

And thy provision never fails.

In thee, O Lord, we find our daily bread,

For thou art the source of all nourishment,

Thou dost satisfy the hungry soul,

And give strength to the weary traveler.

We acknowledge thee as our sustainer,

For in thy mercy, thou dost provide moment by moment,

Thou dost clothe the lilies of the field,

And feed the birds of the air,

How much more wilt thou provide for thy beloved children.

We long, O Lord, for hearts of contentment and gratitude,

That we may be thankful for all thy blessings,

And cherish thy sustenance hour by hour,

As thou dost provide good gifts.

Remove, O Lord, our anxious thoughts and worries,

For our hearts are often consumed with earthly cares,

Teach us to trust in thee with all our hearts,

And to rely on thy sustenance in times of need.

May we not seek after earthly treasures,

But set our minds on things above,

For thou art the true sustainer of our souls,

And in thee alone do we find true satisfaction.

O Lord, in thy boundless provision, hear our prayer,

And let thy name be made known to all the earth,

For thou art the God who sustains thy creation,

Now and forevermore. Amen.

The Transcendence of God

O Most High and Holy Lord,

Thou art exalted above all creation,

Thy greatness surpasses our understanding,

And thy glory fills the heavens and the earth.

Thou dwellest in unapproachable light,

And thy majesty is beyond compare,

Thou art truly and exceedingly above all,

Which every knee shall bow and every tongue confess.

In thee, O Lord, we behold the splendor of thy holiness,

And tremble at the magnitude of thy power,

For thou art the Almighty God, the Ancient of Days,

Whose throne is established on high.

Forgive us, O Lord, for our minds cannot comprehend thee,

We often forget the transcendence of thy being,

Teach us to approach thee with reverence and awe,

And to worship thee in spirit and in truth.

May our lives be a reflection of thy transcendent goodness,

And may we proclaim thy greatness to the ends of the earth,

For thou art high above all we see and know,

Beyond what our mortal minds can comprehend.

We seek, O Lord, hearts of humility and contrition,

That we may acknowledge thee as the true Holy One,

And bow before thee in adoration and praise,

For thou art exalted far above all gods.

O Lord, in thy transcendent majesty, hear our prayer,

And let thy name be exalted above all names,

For thou art the Most High God,

Whose glory fills the earth. Amen.

The Unity of God

O glorious Three-in-One,

Thou art the One True God,

Whose essence is indivisible,

And whose nature is perfect harmony.

In thee, O Lord, we find the source of all unity,

For thou art the Creator of all things,

And in thee, all things hold together,

In perfect order and divine symmetry.

Thou hast revealed thy unity in the mystery of the Trinity,

Father, Son, and Holy Spirit,

Three persons, yet one God,

In perfect communion and mutual love.

Absolve us, O Lord, from our divisions and discord,

For our hearts are often filled with strife and contention,

Teach us to pursue unity and peace,

And to live in harmony with one another.

Let our lives be a reflection of thy divine unity,

And may we bear witness to the world of thy love and grace,

For thou dost unite all things in heaven and on earth,

Through the saving work of thy Son and thy Spirit.

Fill us, O Lord, with hearts of understanding and forbearance,

That we may seek the good of others above our own,

And strive for the unity of the Spirit in the bond of peace,

For thou art the God of peace and unity.

O Lord, in thy perfect unity, hear our prayer,

And let thy Spirit dwell richly in our hearts,

For thou art the One True God,

Who unites all, now and forevermore. Amen.

The Wisdom of God

O Wonderful and Wise God,

Thou art the source of all wisdom,

Whose understanding is infinite,

And whose ways are beyond our comprehension.

With wisdom thou hast laid the foundations of the earth,

And established the heavens with understanding,

In thy wisdom, thou dost govern all things,

And order them according to thy perfect will.

We come before thee, O Lord, with hearts full of awe,

For thou art the Ancient of Days,

And thy wisdom surpasses all understanding,

Thy plans are unsearchable, and thy ways are past finding out.

We seek, O Lord, hearts of wisdom and discernment,

That we may walk in thy word and follow thy precepts,

And may we seek after wisdom as hidden treasure,

For thou dost give wisdom generously to all who ask.

Cleanse us, O Lord, of our pride and arrogance,

For thinking that we can comprehend thy ways,

Teach us to humbly submit to thy wisdom,

And to trust in thy will in all things.

May we never lean on our own understanding,

But may we acknowledge thee in all our ways,

And submit ourselves to thy sovereign rule,

For we see only through a glass, dimly.

O Lord, in thy perfect understanding, hear our prayer,

And grant unto us the discernment to know thy will,

For thou art the source of all wisdom,

Now and forevermore. Amen.

The Wrath of God

O God of Wrath,
Thou art the only righteous Judge,
Whose wrath is kindled against all unrighteousness,
And whose justice demands recompense for sin.

We come before thee, O Lord, with trembling hearts,
For we have sinned against thee in thought, word, and deed,
And we acknowledge that we deserve thy righteous judgment.

Thou hast warned us of thy wrath against sin,
And thou hast declared that the wages of sin is death,
We have provoked thy anger with our rebellion,
And have incurred the penalty of thy holy law.

We beg forgive us, O Lord, for our willful disobedience,
For our hearts are deceitful and desperately wicked,
Have mercy upon us, O God, according to thy lovingkindness,
And blot out our transgressions for thy name's sake.

Let thy wrath be turned away from us, O Lord,

And may we be spared from the punishment we deserve,

For thou hast provided a way of escape through thy Son,

Who bore the penalty for our sins upon the cross.

Place in us, O Lord, hearts of contrition and humility,

That we may turn from our wicked ways,

And seek thy face with repentant hearts,

For thou art slow to anger and abundant in mercy.

O Lord, in thy mercy, hear our prayer,

And let thy grace and compassion overshadow thy wrath,

For thou art also the God of mercy and forgiveness,

Whose wrath shall be satisfied, now and forevermore. Amen.

Afterword

I hope that the prayers in this book have encouraged you, drawn you closer to the Lord, and given you thoughts to meditate on throughout your day. In our busy age, the discipline of prayer is needed more than ever.

If you have found these prayers beneficial, please consider leaving a review or sharing with someone who you think may enjoy them.

May God bless you abundantly.

Made in the USA
Columbia, SC
10 April 2024

34193976R00050